MY FIRST *Prayer* BOOK

TREASURE PRESS

Previously published in 1975 by
Lion Publishing as *Everyday Graces, Everyday Prayers, Goodnight Prayers* and *Prayers for Special Days*

This edition published in 1988 by
Treasure Press
59 Grosvenor Street
London W1

ISBN 1 85051 320 1

Printed by Mandarin Offset in Hong Kong

Prayers for Special Days

Illustrated by Jill Barklem

Sunday

For this new Sunday with its light,
For rest and shelter of the night,
We thank you, heavenly Father.
Through this new week but just begun,
Be near, and help us every one
To please you, heavenly Father.

A Happy Day

Thank you for each happy day,
For fun, for friends,
and work and play;
Thank you for your loving care,
Here at home and everywhere.

Today

Dear Lord Jesus, we shall have this day only once; before it is gone, help us to do all the good we can, so that today is not a wasted day.

My Birthday

O loving God, today is my birthday. For your care from the day I was born until today and for your love, I thank you. Help me to be strong and healthy, and to show love for others, as Jesus did.

Autumn Days

All good gifts around us
Are sent from heaven above;
Then thank the Lord,
O thank the Lord,
For all his love.

Thank you, our heavenly Father for harvest time: for ripe fruit in the orchards and berries in the hedges: for the vegetable harvest and all the food gathered in and stored for winter days.

A Spoilt Day

O God, you made us and you love us, thank you for being so willing to forgive us. Make us quick to own up to you whenever we do wrong, so that we may quickly be forgiven. Then our day will not be spoilt by worry and we can be happy all day long, through Jesus Christ our Lord.

Holidays

Loving Father, on this day
Make us happy in our play,
Kind and helpful, playing fair,
Letting others have a share.

Thank you, God, for holidays
In the lovely summer days,
For our picnics, for our fun,
For our playing in the sun.
Make us good, with smiling faces,
So our homes are friendly places,
And the helpful things we do
Make all our mothers happy too.

Acknowledgments
'For this new Sunday with its light' from *A Brownie Guide Prayer Book* by Rosalie Wakefield, SPCK. 'O Loving God' from *Children's Prayers from Other Lands*, Curtis Brown Ltd. 'Thank you, our heavenly Father' from *Ladybird Book of Prayers Through the Year* by H. I. Rostron, Ladybird Books Ltd. 'O God, you made us' from *Prayers for Today's Church* by Dick Williams, Church Pastoral-Aid Society. 'Loving Father, on this day' by D. M. Prescott from *The Infant Teacher's Prayer Book*, Blandford Press. 'Thank you, God, for holidays' by Irene Taylor and Phyllis Garlick from *All Our Days*, Church Missionary Society

Everyday Prayers

Illustrated by Gillian Gaze

Sunday

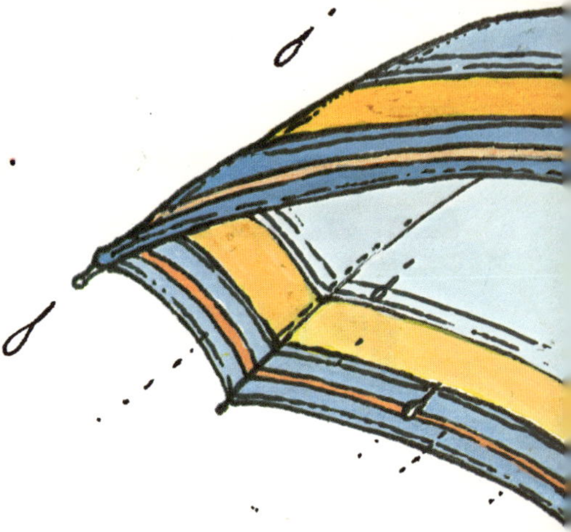

Grant, O heavenly Father,
that I may be glad
through all this day:
Glad that you are our Father,
and that you love us;
Glad that we can always be sure
of your help;
Glad that we can serve you
by helping other people.
This is the day that you have made,
and I will rejoice
and be glad in it.

Monday

Father, thank you for the night,
And for the pleasant morning light;
For rest and food and loving care,
And all that makes the day so fair.
Help me to do the things I should,
To be to others kind and good;
In all I do at work or play
To grow more loving every day.

Tuesday

Jesus, may I be like you;
Loving, kind in all I do;
Kind and happy when I play
Close beside you all the day.

Heavenly Father,
you have given this new day to me.
Help me to make it one
that pleases you by doing my best
in everything, because I love you.

Wednesday

Thank you, God, for this new day
In my school to work and play.
Please be with me all day long,
In every story, game and song.
May all the happy things we do
Make you, our Father, happy too.

Thursday

Thank you, Lord Jesus,
that you love us the same today
as yesterday.

Lord Jesus, I pray for those
who will be unhappy today:
for mothers who have no food
to cook for their children;
for fathers who cannot earn
enough money for their families;
for children who are sick
or frightened;
and for those who are alone
and without people to love them.

Friday

Thank you, God, for the day-time
when I can be awake and busy.
Thank you for all there is
for me to do today:
new things to find out,
friends and games to play with.
Thank you for the sun
that gives us warmth and light
to see by.

Saturday

For this new morning with its light,
Father, I thank you.
For rest and shelter of the night,
Father, I thank you;
For health and food,
for love and friends
For everything your goodness sends,
Father in heaven, I thank you.

Acknowledgments
'Grant, O heavenly Father' by Brenda Holloway from *Prayers for the Home*, Hodder and Stoughton Ltd. 'Jesus, may I be like you' from *Hymns and Songs for Children*, National Society. 'Thank you, God, for this new day' by D. M. Prescott from *The Infant Teacher's Prayer Book*, Blandford Press. 'Thank you, Lord Jesus', 'Lord Jesus, I pray for those' and 'Thank you, God, for the day-time' by Zinnia Bryan from *Let's Talk to God*, Scripture Union.

Goodnight Prayers

Illustrated by Gillian Gaze

Sunday

Father, unto you we raise
Hearts and voices full of praise.
Bless us waking, guard us sleeping,
Through this night and all our days.

Monday

Glory to thee, my God, this night
For all the blessings of the light;
Keep me, O keep me, King of kings,
Beneath thy own almighty wings.

Tuesday

Jesus, tender Shepherd, hear me;
Bless your little lamb tonight;
Through the darkness
please be near me;
Keep me safe till morning light.

All this day your hand has led me,
And I thank you for your care;
You have warmed and clothed
and fed me;
Listen to my evening prayer.

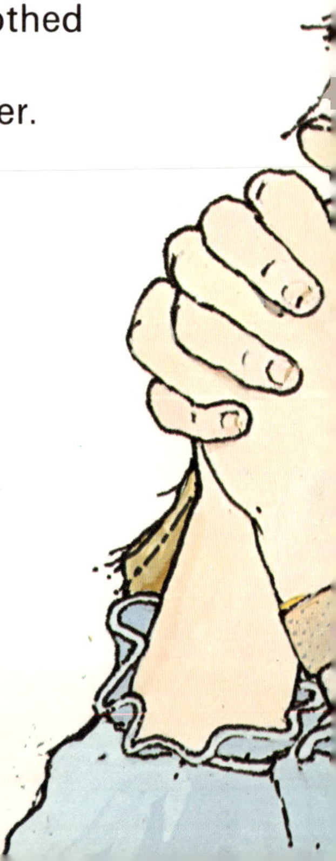

Wednesday

O God, our heavenly Father,
bless and keep your children
all over the world,
this night and for ever.

Thursday

Jesus, friend of little children,
Be a friend to me;
Take my hand and ever keep me
Close to thee.

Friday

Loving Father, I'm sorry
for the wrong things that I have
said or thought or done today.
I'm sorry if I made others unhappy,
but most of all, help me
to be sorry if I have hurt you.

God the Father, bless us;
God the Son, defend us;
God the Spirit, keep us
Now and evermore.

Saturday

In our work and play God leads us,
Every step we take.
In our sleep he will be near us,
Watching till we wake.

Acknowledgments
'Jesus, friend of little children' by W. J. Mathams from *Songs of Praise*, Oxford University Press. 'Loving Father, I'm sorry' by Zinnia Bryan from *Let's Talk to God*, Scripture Union.

Everyday Graces

Illustrated by Gillian Gaze

Sunday

Thank you for the world so sweet,
Thank you for the food we eat.
Thank you for the birds that sing,
Thank you, God, for everything.

Monday

All good gifts around us
Are sent from heaven above.
Then thank the Lord,
O thank the Lord
For all his love.

Thank you, Jesus,
for this food.
Amen.

Tuesday

God is great, God is good,
Thank you, God, for all our food.

Wednesday

For every cup and plateful,
God make us truly grateful.

For health and strength
and daily food
we praise your name
O Lord.

Thursday

For food and drink and happy days,
Accept our gratitude and praise;
In serving others, Lord, we do
Express our thankfulness to you.

Friday

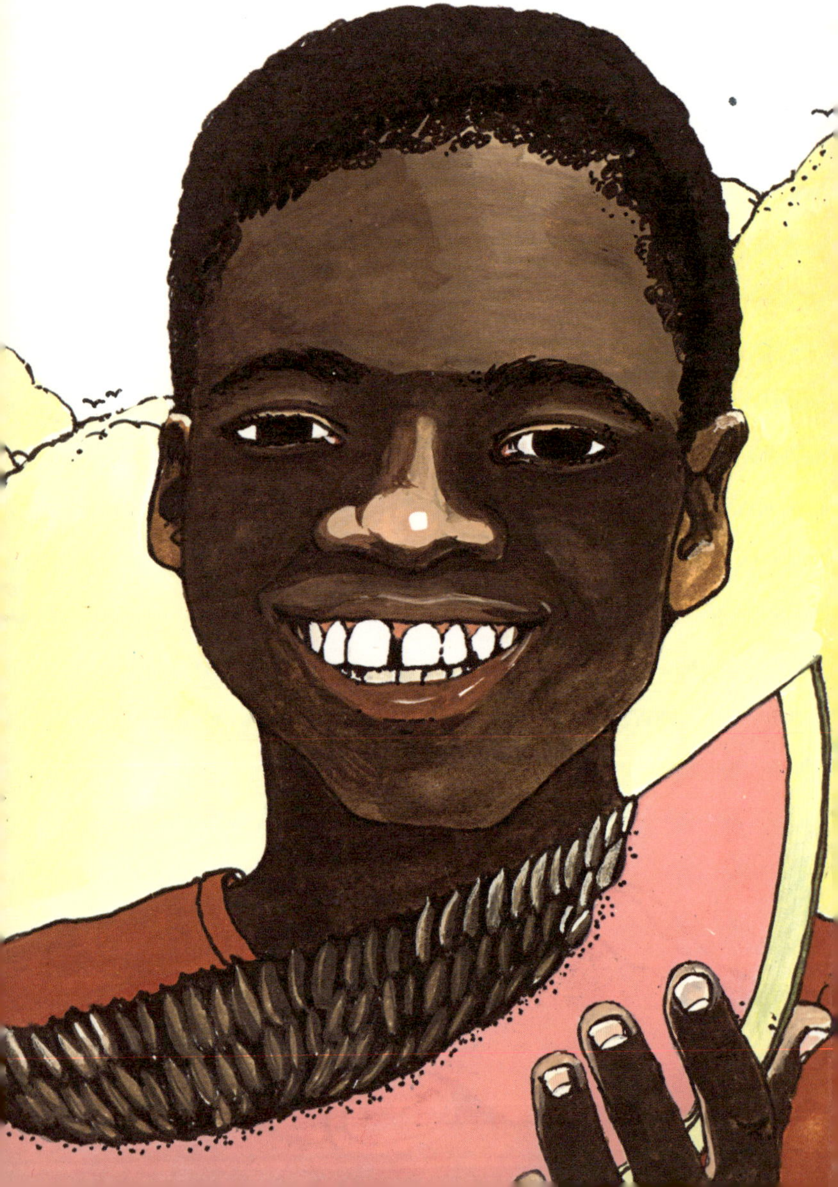

We thank you,
Father, for your care
For all your children everywhere.
As you feed us all our days
May our lives be filled with praise.

Saturday

Praise God
from whom all blessings flow,
Praise him,
all creatures here below,
Praise him above,
you heavenly host,
Praise Father,
Son and Holy Ghost.

Acknowledgments

'Thank you for the world so sweet' by E. Rutter Leatham from *Hymns and Songs for Children*, The National Society. 'God is great, God is good' and 'For food and drink and happy days' from *Little Folded Hands*, Concordia Publishing House Ltd. 'For every cup and plateful' from *An Anthology of Prayers* by A. S. T. Fisher, Longman Group Ltd. 'For health and strength', J. Curwen and Sons. 'We thank you, Father, for your care' by Rosalie Wakefield from *A Brownie Guide Prayer Book*, SPCK.